Food and Recipes of the Revolutionary War

George Erdosh

The Rosen Publishing Group's
PowerKids Press™
New York

The recipes in this book are intended for a child to make together with an adult.

Many thanks to Ruth Rosen and her test kitchen.

Published in 1997 by The Rosen Publishing Group, Inc.
29 East 21st Street, New York, NY 10010

First Edition

Book Design: Danielle Primiceri

Photo Credits: Cover (right) © Bettmann, (left) © Orion/International Stock; pp. 4, 7, 12 (top), 18 (top), 20 (middle) © Bettmann; p. 8 (bottom) © James Davis/International Stock; pp. 8 (top), 15, 16, 18 (middle) © Joe Viesti/Viesti Associates, Inc.; pp. 10, 20 (top) © Corbis-Bettmann.

Photo Illustrations: pp. 12 (middle, bottom), 18 (middle, bottom), 20 (middle, bottom) by Ira Fox; pp. 9, 13, 19, 21 by Christine Innamorato and Olga Vega.

Contents

Freedom at Last

Joseph was nine years old in 1775. This was an exciting time in American history. It was the year the American **colonists** (KOL-un-ists) decided to free themselves from British rule. It was also the beginning of the **Revolutionary** (rev-uh-LOO-shun-ayr-ee) War.

England had placed many rules on the American **colonies** (KOL-un-eez). For example, everything that the colonists wanted to buy from or sell to other countries had to go through England first. That way England made money on whatever the colonists bought or sold.

By 1775, the colonists had decided they wanted to rule themselves. For one thing, they wanted to be able to buy and sell their own foods and goods. The Revolutionary War began shortly after that, and it lasted for eight years.

◄ *Food played an important part in the start of the Revolutionary War.*

Food of the Time

Before the American Revolution, most people were farmers, like Joseph's family. Even some people who lived in the cities had gardens, raised chickens, had a cow or a goat for milk, and sometimes even a pig. Important members of government, such as George Washington and Thomas Jefferson, had large farms on which they grew much of the food they ate. Nearly everyone ate well. Visitors to the colonies were amazed to see so many different kinds of food and so much of it. To many people's surprise, there was even enough for food most people throughout the war.

Because so many people had farms on which they grew their own food, few people went hungry during the Revolutionary War. ▶

Breakfast

Around the time of the war, many colonists ate big breakfasts every day. Joseph usually had oatmeal or cornmeal mush with bread and butter. His mother also served some sort of meat, such as beef steaks, **mutton** (MUT-ten) chops, veal cutlets, or sausages. In some places, a dish called scrapple was often served with eggs. Scrapple was a cornmeal dish made with bits of pork or sausage.

In the northern colonies, people also ate pancakes with maple syrup. In the Southern colonies, people often ate hot rolls, biscuits, and muffins. Like many colonists at that time, Joseph's parents drank coffee rather than tea, which was the **traditional** (truh-DISH-un-ul) drink.

Tea was one of the foods that the colonists **imported** (im-POR-ted) from other countries. But in 1773, England placed a **tax** (TAKS) on tea and other imported goods. The colonists were so angry about having to pay tax on tea, many people stopped drinking it. They drank coffee instead.

Frumenty

1 cup bulgur wheat
1 cup boiling water
¼ teaspoon salt
½ cup milk
½ cup half-and-half
½ teaspoon
    cinnamon
⅛ teaspoon ground
    mace
2 tablespoons
    brown sugar

HOW TO DO IT:

☞ Put the bulgur wheat and salt in a small bowl.
☞ Pour in the boiling water and stir. Cover and let sit for 15 minutes.
☞ In a medium-size pot, heat the milk and half-and-half on medium heat.
☞ Add the cinnamon, mace, and brown sugar.
☞ Stir, and don't let the mixture boil.
☞ When the mixture is hot, add the soaked bulgur wheat and stir well.
☞ Cook and stir this porridge for 10 minutes. Serve. This serves three people.

Frumenty was an English breakfast food made from wheat. It was eaten by many colonists in the North. Frumenty was cooked for a long time because wheat is a tough grain. But today we use bulgur wheat, which is already cooked. All we need to do it is soak the bulgur. You can find bulgur in many supermarkets and in most health food stores.

A Snack After School

Joseph was hungry and thirsty as he walked home from school. When he got home, his mother was waiting for him with his usual snack: a piece of bread that Joseph dipped in warm beer.

This seems like a strange snack today. But during colonial times, water and milk were not safe to drink if you lived in a city. Milk spoiled quickly if it was not kept cool, and there were no **refrigerators** (ree-FRID-jer-ay-terz) yet. People could buy fresh milk if someone in the neighborhood owned a cow or a goat, but not everyone did. And in most cities, waste was allowed to flow into the drinking water. That made the water bad to drink. So people usually drank beer, apple juice, and apple cider.

◀ *During the Revolutionary War, kids had to walk to and from school. For some kids, this meant walking several miles each way.*

11

Good Food, Bad Health

During this time, people ate a lot of food, but they didn't eat food that was very good for them. Most people didn't know much about **nutrition** (new-TRISH-un). They ate meat with a lot of fat on it. They often ate cream and butter, which has a lot fat in it too. Nobody ate raw vegetables, and few people ate enough fruit. Joseph's mother boiled all their vegetables. She often cooked them for so long that they lost all their **vitamins** (VY-ta-menz). "Salad" at that time meant any green vegetable that could be cooked and eaten.

Many people became sick because they didn't eat nutritious foods or cook foods in a way that was good for them. Today, we eat many of the same foods that the colonists ate. But we've learned how to cook them so they are nutritious.

Revolutionary Boiled Salad

You will need:

1 10-oz package frozen chopped spinach, defrosted

¼ cup raisins

2 tablespoons butter

2 tablespoons white vinegar

1½ teaspoons brown sugar

½ teaspoon salt

HOW TO DO IT:

☞ Drain the spinach in a colander and put it in a medium-sized pot.

☞ Cover the pot and put it on the stove, and turn the heat to medium.

☞ Cook the spinach for five minutes, stirring it a few times.

☞ Uncover the pot. With a large spoon, stir in the raisins, butter, vinegar, brown sugar and salt.

☞ Keep cooking for five more minutes, stirring it from time to time.

☞ Serve as a vegetable dish, not as a salad.

This serves two people.

Sweet Things

Like many people, Joseph loved sweets. His mother served something sweet at almost every meal. Many of these sweets were made from maple sugar, maple syrup, or dried fruit. At that time, sugar was expensive. In the northern colonies people tapped maple trees for the sap, which they turned into maple syrup and maple sugar. In areas where there were no maple trees, people made sweets with dried fruits. Joseph's mother served jellies, jams, or sweet fruit sauces with their meat. For dessert, she made pies, puddings, and tarts. Some people even ate ice cream during the winter, when there was plenty of snow and ice to make it.

Apples were a favorite food of many colonists and were used to make pie, sauce, juice, and cider. They were also dried and eaten as a ▶ sweet treat or made into dried apple pie during the winter.

Soldier Food

Joseph's father was a **minuteman** (MIN-it-man) in the army during the Revolutionary War. Along with many other colonial men, Joseph's father **volunteered** (vol-un-TEERD) to fight in the war. He wrote letters to his family telling them what the war was like.

Joseph's father said that most soldiers received daily **rations** (RASH-enz) of food. Their rations usually included a large piece of pork or beef, flour or cornmeal, dried peas or beans, and coffee. They had to cook all the food, even bread, over campfires. A group of six or eight men chose one man to do the cooking. When they got tired of his cooking, they all voted for a new cook.

◀ *Most American soldiers were well fed throughout the Revolutionary War.*

17

Army Cooking

Each group of six or eight soldiers had one heavy, iron kettle for cooking. Officers also had their own kettles, but their kettles had lids. This meant that officers could cook their food faster than soldiers could.

The army told the soldiers to make stew with the meat. The army doctors believed that frying, baking, or broiling were unhealthy ways to cook meat. Officers often checked the camps to make sure that the soldiers cooked meat "the healthy way." But the soldiers loved the taste of meat when it was broiled over an open fire or fried in fat. When the officers weren't around, they often cooked their meat that way.

Minuteman's Beef Stew

You will need:

1½ pound beef chuck roast

2 tablespoons vegetable oil

1 14.5 or 16-ounce can beef broth

½ teaspoon salt

½ teaspoon ground black pepper

1 bay leaf

1 medium onion

1 clove garlic

1 medium potato

2 carrots

HOW TO DO IT:

☞ Cut the meat into bite-sized pieces.

☞ Heat the oil in a large, heavy pot on medium-high heat. Gently add the pieces of meat.

☞ Stir with a large spoon until the meat is brown all over. This will take ten minutes.

☞ Pour the beef broth over the meat and lower the heat under the pot. Add salt, pepper, and bay leaf.

☞ Wait until the broth starts to boil, stir, then cover the pot and simmer on low heat for one hour.

☞ While the beef is cooking, peel and chop the onion into small pieces.

☞ Peel and mince the garlic. Peel the potato and carrots and cut them into bite-size pieces.

☞ After the beef has simmered for an hour, add the onion, garlic, potatoes, and carrots, bring it to a boil over low heat.

☞ Cover the pot and simmer for 30 minutes more.

☞ Serve the stew with bread and butter.

This serves four to five people.

Enough Food During the War

Most people ate well, even during the war. There were a few times when people who lived in cities could not buy some foods because the army needed those foods for the soldiers. But that wasn't very often. Joseph and his family continued to eat two large meals a day—the first for breakfast, and the second around noon. They usually ate a light meal of bread and butter in the evening.

Boston Baked Beans

You will need:

6 cups canned
   navy beans
1 medium onion
1 tablespoon dry
   mustard powder
1 teaspoon ground
   black pepper
1½ teaspoons salt
1½ tablespoons
   white vinegar
¼ cup molasses
1 piece smoked pork
   shoulder, neck, or
   ham bone

HOW TO DO IT:

☞ Preheat the oven to 250° F.
☞ Chop the onion into small pieces.
☞ Mix dry mustard, pepper, salt, vinegar, and molasses in a small bowl.
☞ Mix all the ingredients together in a large, heavy baking pan with a lid.
☞ Add enough water to cover the beans. Stir again. Make sure the pork bone is under the liquid.
☞ Put the lid on the pan and put the pan in the oven.
☞ Bake for five hours. Stir beans at least twice during the baking. If the beans seem dry, add a little water.
☞ Thirty minutes before beans are finished baking, take off the lid. Continue to bake uncovered.
☞ When finished, take the pot out of the oven and serve the beans with cornbread.
This serves six people.

The colonists learned to cook beans this way from the Native Americans. It is still a popular dish, and this recipe hasn't changed much since colonial times.

Food After the War

Joseph was seventeen years old by the time the war ended in 1783. In the newly-formed United States, there was more food and more variety than ever before. This was especially true in cities, such as New York City, where people from all over the world came to live. These people brought their own cultures, ideas about food, and ways of cooking.

Joseph took a trip to New York City with his father. He couldn't believe his eyes when he visited a market there. He counted 77 kinds of fish and seafood, 52 kinds of meat and poultry, and 27 kinds of vegetables and fruits. Some people thought that Americans ate too much or wasted food. But most Americans simply enjoyed their food, and ate a lot of it.

Glossary

colonist (KOL-un-ist) A person who moves to a new land, but stays under the rule of his old country.

colony (KOL-un-ee) An area of land settled by people from another country and that remains under the rule of that country.

import (IM-port) To bring in from another country.

minuteman (MIN-it-man) A person who volunteered to fight in the Revolutionary War, and who could be "ready to march in a minute."

mutton (MUT-ten) The meat of a sheep.

nutrition (new-TRISH-un) Anything that a living thing needs for energy, to grow, or to heal.

ration (RASH-en) A fixed amount of food given to a person.

refrigerator (ree-FRID-jer-ay-ter) A machine that is used to make or keep things cold.

revolutionary (rev-uh-LOO-shun-ayr-ee) Of or having to do with a complete change in government.

tax (TAKS) Money given by the people to the government.

traditional (truh-DISH-un-ul) A way of doing something that is passed down from parent to child.

vitamin (VY-ta-men) A nutrient that helps your body fight illness and grow strong.

volunteer (vol-un-TEER) To offer to do something for free.

Index

DATE DUE